I Know Someone with a
Hearing Impairment

Vic Parker

www.raintreepublishers.co.uk
Visit our website to find out
more information about
Raintree books.

To order:
☎ Phone 0845 6044371
🖹 Fax +44 (0) 1865 312263
🖥 Email myorders@raintreepublishers.co.uk

Customers from outside the UK please telephone +44 1865 312262

Raintree is an imprint of Capstone Global Library
Limited, a company incorporated in England and
Wales having its registered office at 7 Pilgrim Street,
London, EC4V 6LB – Registered company number:
6695582

Text © Capstone Global Library Limited 2011
First published in hardback in 2011
The moral rights of the proprietor have been asserted.

Edited by Rebecca Rissman, Dan Nunn,
    and Catherine Veitch
Designed by Steve Mead and Joanna Hinton Malivoire
Picture research by Tracy Cummins
Originated by Capstone Global Library
Printed and bound in China by Leo Paper Products Ltd

ISBN 978 1 406 22081 0
15 14 13 12 11
10 9 8 7 6 5 4 3 2 1

British Library Cataloguing in Publication Data
Parker, Victoria.
I know someone with a hearing impairment. –
(Understanding health issues)
617.8-dc22
A full catalogue record for this book is available from
the British Library.

Acknowledgements
We would like to thank the following for permission to
reproduce photographs: Corbis pp. **8** (© Randy Faris),
9 (© ER productions Ltd/Blend Images), **24** (© Vicky
Alhadeff/Lebrecht Music & Arts), **27** (© Mark Edward
Atkinson/Blend Images); Getty Images pp. **11** (David
Sacks), **14** (Patryce Bak), **19** (Huntstock), **23** (UpperCut
Images), **25** (NBAE/David Liam Kyle); istockphoto
pp. **5** (© Zhang Bo), **12** (© Darko Novakovic), **18**
(© pierredesvarre); Photo Researchers, Inc. pp. **13**
(AJPhoto), **21** (APHP-PSL-GARO / PHANIE), **22** (Penny
Tweedie); Photolibrary p. **20** (Chapman Wiedelphoto);
Shutterstock pp. **4** (© Patricia Hofmeester), **10** (© juan
carlos tinjaca), **15** (© MaszaS), **16** (©Paul Matthew
Photography); ZUMA Press p. **17** (Monterey Herald).

Cover photograph of Lu Zhiyan at Kuangyuan Hearing
and Speaking Convalescence Centre, Zhengzhou
reproduced with permission of Zuma Press
(Zhu Xiang/Xinhua).

We would like to thank Ashley Wolinski and Matthew
Siegel for their invaluable help in the preparation of
this book.

Every effort has been made to contact copyright
holders of any material reproduced in this book. Any
omissions will be rectified in subsequent printings if
notice is given to the publisher.

All the Internet addresses (URLs) given in this book
were valid at the time of going to press. However, due
to the ... ...es
may h...
cease...nd
publis...
reade...be
accep...

Contents

Do you know someone with a hearing
   impairment? 4

What is a hearing impairment? 6

Blocked ears 8

Damaged ears 10

Who gets a hearing impairment? 12

Living with a hearing impairment 14

Hearing aids and implants. 16

Lip-reading and sign language 18

At school and university 20

At home and going out 22

Famous people 24

Being a good friend 26

Hearing impairments – facts and fiction 28

Glossary 30

Find out more 31

Index 32

Some words are printed in bold, **like this**. You can
find out what they mean in the glossary.

Do you know someone with a hearing impairment?

We use our ears and **brains** to hear sound and make sense of it. You may have a friend with a hearing **impairment**. This means they hear differently or not as well as others.

You cannot see sound, but you can feel it if you speak against a balloon.

Some people with hearing impairments can speak as clearly as people without.

Often, you cannot see that people have hearing impairments. However, you may be able to tell by the way they talk. People who have never heard sound often do not say words as others do.

What is a hearing impairment?

Our ears are made up of three main parts: the outside part of your ear catches sound, the middle part makes sound louder, and the inside part sends messages to the **brain**. The brain makes sense of the sound.

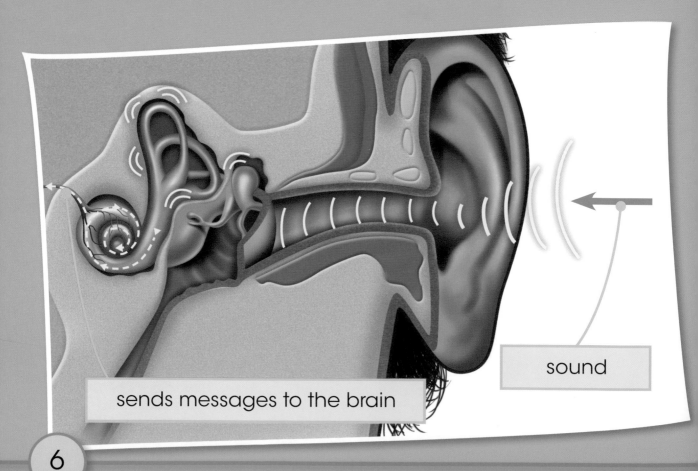

sends messages to the brain

sound

If there is a problem with any part of the ear, or the part of the brain that makes sense of hearing, a hearing **impairment** happens.

Hearing impairments can be different for different people:

- some people can hear some sounds but not others
- some people cannot hear any sounds at all. They are said to be **deaf**.
- it can affect one ear or both
- if both, one ear may be worse than the other.

Blocked ears

Sometimes a hearing **impairment** happens because sound cannot travel properly into the outside or middle of the ear. This might be because the ear is blocked.

Illnesses and infections can block the outside or the middle of the ear.

This type of hearing loss can often be made better by taking medicines such as ear drops to clear up the **infection**, or by having an **operation**.

If you have to go into hospital for an operation, you will be well looked after.

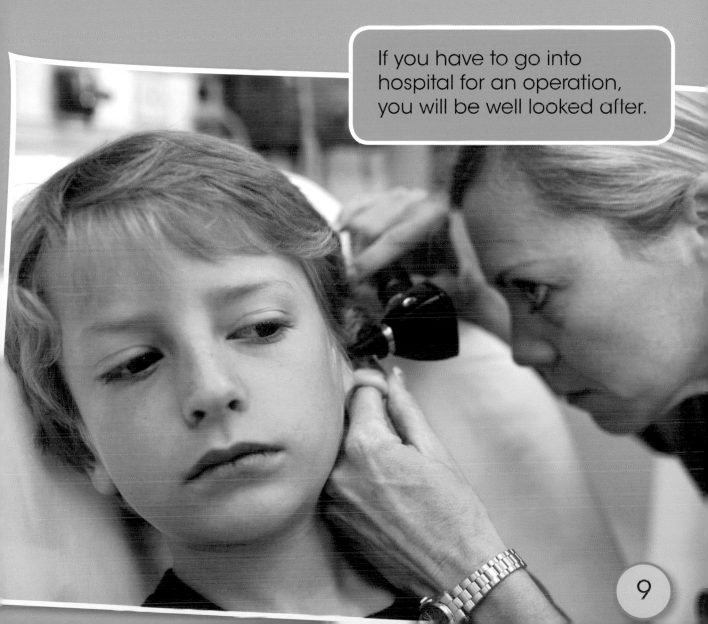

Damaged ears

Some types of hearing damage can run in families.

Sometimes a person loses their hearing because their ear, or the part of the **brain** to do with hearing, is damaged. This means that they cannot hear sound clearly or make sense of it.

This type of hearing loss does not go away. People with damaged hearing can learn to communicate by developing certain skills using special equipment.

Some hearing-impaired people can dance to music by feeling the movements made by **sound waves**.

Who gets a hearing impairment?

Some people are born with hearing **impairments**. Other people can lose their hearing later in life. Hearing loss can happen at any time, to anyone. It can come on slowly or be sudden, such as after a **head injury**.

Hearing loss can happen slowly because a person has been listening to music that is too loud.

Doctors can do tests to check for a hearing impairment. The tests often involve listening for sounds through special headphones.

Many people develop hearing loss as they grow older.

Living with a hearing impairment

People with hearing **impairments** face lots of challenges each day. They may not realize when people are talking to them, or hear a telephone when it rings. They may not hear traffic or doorbells.

People with hearing impairments can have special alarm clocks which go under their pillow and shake very fast when it is time to wake up.

People with hearing impairments can be good at many different sports.

However, there are many ways people with hearing impairments can overcome some of the difficulties they face. People with hearing impairments can live full, happy lives.

Hearing aids and implants

Some people can hear better if they wear a **hearing aid**. A hearing aid fits either inside or behind the ear. Hearing aids make sounds louder and clearer.

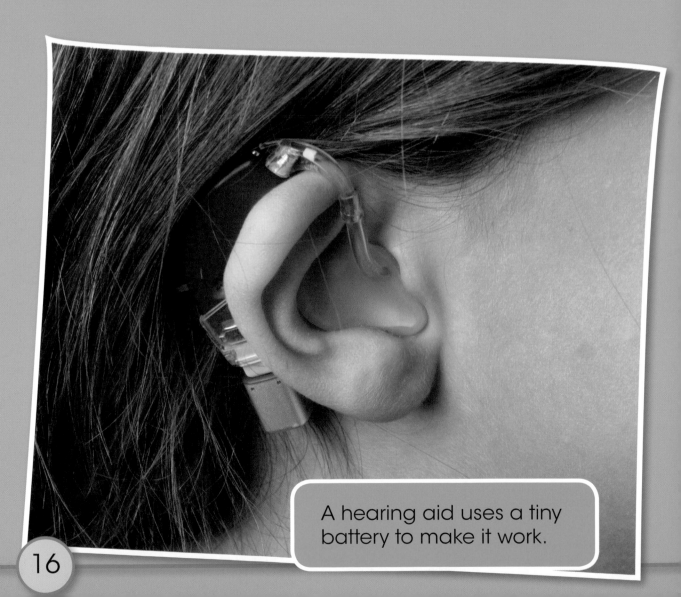

A hearing aid uses a tiny battery to make it work.

This kind of hearing aid does the job of the inner ear.

Other people use a kind of hearing aid that comes in two parts. One part sits outside the ear. The other part is placed under the skin and behind the ear. A doctor puts this in during an **operation**.

Lip-reading and sign language

Some people who are hearing impaired learn to lip-read. This is when they watch the mouth of someone who is talking and recognize the words they are saying from the shape of the mouth and lips.

Lip-readers watch face and body movements to understand what is being said.

People who can hear can also learn sign language.

Many also learn to communicate using sign language. This is when they move their hands and face in a certain way to talk to other people. People can use sign language to build friendships and their confidence at the same time.

At school and university

Some children go to special schools for the hearing impaired, but others go to ordinary schools. A teacher can wear a special microphone that allows a pupil to hear better through a **device** they wear.

A child with a hearing impairment can have a classroom assistant who knows sign language.

People with hearing impairments can do well at university.

Special computer programmes can help people with hearing **impairments** at school, too. These can pick up a teacher's speech and change it into words on the screen that the student can then read.

At home and going out

At home, people with hearing **impairments** can have flashing lights fitted instead of doorbells and alarms. They can have telephones that show what is being spoken. On television, speech can be shown as words on screen.

Dogs can be trained to let a person know when they hear certain sounds, such as a baby crying.

There is no reason for hearing-impaired people to be left out of any fun activity.

People with hearing impairments can enjoy going to the cinema, theatre, concerts, and exhibitions. These places often have special performances where speech appears on a screen.

Famous people

Evelyn Glennie has been **deaf** since the age of twelve. However, she is a famous musician. She performs barefoot, so she can feel the **sound waves** on the stage.

Evelyn Glennie performs in more than a hundred concerts each year.

24

Lance Allred is just one of many successful sportspeople who have a hearing **impairment**.

American Lance Allred was born with almost complete hearing loss. However, he became a basketball player with the US National Basketball Association's Cleveland Cavaliers.

Being a good friend

There are many ways you can be a good friend to someone with a hearing **impairment**, such as:

- blocking your ears with ear plugs for a while to see what a hearing impairment is like

- not speaking extra loudly or slowly to your friend, unless they have asked you to

- if your friend lip-reads, making sure they can see your mouth when you talk.

We all have different bodies and personalities.

Living with a hearing impairment can be difficult at times. But there are many other ways in which we are all different. A good friend likes us just as we are.

Hearing impairments – facts and fiction

Facts

- Millions of people around the world have hearing **impairments**.

- Some **hearing aids** are so small and well-hidden that people don't even notice when someone is wearing one.

Fiction

(?) If you start to lose your hearing, you will know about it.

WRONG! Other people may notice someone's hearing becoming impaired before they do.

(?) Hearing impairment is always about sound not being loud enough.

WRONG! In many kinds of hearing impairment, people cannot hear high sounds, rather than just quiet sounds. This can make it difficult for them to hear speech in noisy places.

Glossary

brain body part inside your skull that controls all other parts of your body and that helps you to think

deaf an impairment which causes a loss of hearing. Someone can be totally or partly deaf.

device small piece of special equipment

head injury damage to the head caused by an accident, such as falling or being hit by something

hearing aid special equipment that helps a person to hear

impairment condition that stops part of your body from working correctly

infection an illness

operation type of medical treatment carried out in a hospital by a special doctor called a surgeon

sound waves sound travels through the air in invisible waves. Even though you cannot see them, you can sometimes feel them.

Find out more

Books to read

Jordan Has a Hearing Loss (Like Me Like You),
  Jillian Powell (Evans Books, 2009)
Some Kids Are Deaf (Understanding Differences)
  Lola M. Schaefer (Capstone Press, 2008)
Sound (How Does Science Work?),
  Carol Ballard (Wayland, 2008)

Sound and Hearing (Sounds All Around Us),
  Catherine Veitch (Heinemann Library, 2009)

Websites

**http://kidshealth.org/kid/health_problems/
sight/hearing_impairment.html**
Learn about hearing impairment on
this website.

http://www.hearingdogs.org.uk/
This website is about hearing dogs.

Index

alarm 22
alarm clocks 14

brain 4, 6, 7, 10

computer 21

doctors 13, 17
dogs 22
doorbell 14, 22

ears 4, 6, 7, 8, 10, 16, 17, 26

headphones 13
hearing aid 16, 17, 28

illness 8
infection 8, 9

lip-reading 18, 26

medicines 9
microphone 20
music 11, 12

operation 9, 17

schools 20, 21
screen 21, 23
sign language 19, 20
sound 4, 5, 6, 7, 8, 10, 13, 16, 22, 29
sound waves 11, 24
speak 5
speech 21, 29

talk 5, 14, 19, 26
teacher 20, 21
telephone 14, 22
television 22
traffic 14